Bath Ey

Story by Jacquie Kilkenny
Photography by Lindsay Edwards

Rigby
A Harcourt Achieve Imprint

www.Rigby.com
1-800-531-5015

"Come and have your bath, Clark,"
said Dad.

"I'm not going to have a bath today,"
said Clark.
"I'm clean."

"In you go, Clark," said Dad.

"Your duck can have a bath, too," said Riley.

Clark got into the bathtub.

"Here is your duck," said Riley.

"Look at my duck," said Clark.

"He is swimming.

I can make him

go up and down

in the water like this."

"May I wash your hair, Clark?" said Dad.

"No, Dad," cried Clark.
"The water gets in my eyes."

"I will not let the water get in your eyes," said Dad.

Clark cried and cried. "The water **will** get in my eyes," he said.

Riley went out

of the bathroom.

Riley came back
with some goggles.

"Here are my goggles, Clark,"
said Riley.
"The water will not get
in your eyes now."

"You may wash my hair, Dad,"
said Clark.

"Riley's goggles are my new bath eyes!"